WHOSE RULES?

RAHUL CHANDRAN

To the unheard,
the unseen,
the misunderstood.

To everyone who was told they weren't enough,
and still chose to breathe, love, and continue anyway.

This book is for you.
You are not alone.

Contents

Foreword

We live in a world where we are taught how to look, act, and feel based on rules we never agreed to.

Rules written by society.

Rules enforced by culture.

Rules we carry in silence.

Whose Rules was not written to preach, fix, or diagnose.

It was written because I, like many of you, have lived with the weight of being judged for being skinny, too dark, too emotional, too different. I've battled mental health in silence, watched people suffer from family trauma, and seen toxic relationships glorified on screens while crumbling behind closed doors.

This book is a mirror for anyone who's tired of pretending.

It doesn't promise answers.

But it does offer truth.

And sometimes, that's all we need to feel a little less alone.

— Rahul Chandran

Preface

This book started as pain.

Then it became pages.

I never imagined I'd write something like this. I wasn't looking for sympathy or applause. I just wanted to breathe easier. To finally say the things I kept locked inside.

Whose Rules is not just my story it's everyone's in some way. Each chapter is built on real-life experiences mine, and others I've seen quietly suffer. People who smiled through trauma. Who were mocked for their body, shamed for their feelings, or silenced because their truth was inconvenient.

I wrote this to heal.

If it helps you heal too even a little then this book has done what it was meant to do.

Acknowledgements

To those who listened to me when I couldn't explain what I was feeling thank you.
To those who walked away when I was at my worst thank you too.
Both shaped me into who I am.

To my friends, my readers, my supporters
You gave me the courage to write without filters. To share the raw, the uncomfortable, and the real.

To every soul who shared their story with me even anonymously I see you. You live in these pages.

And finally, to myself:
For surviving.
For speaking.
For choosing to live.

Prologue

They told me to stay strong.
But never taught me how.
They told me to grow up.
But never told me what that actually meant.
They said "real men don't cry,"
"dark skin isn't attractive,"
"love will fix everything,"
"family is everything,"
and "mental health is just overthinking."
I believed them.
Until I broke.
And in that breaking, I saw something clearer than I ever had:
None of these rules were mine.
So I started rewriting them.
And in those rewritten lines, this book was born.
This is not a manual.
It's not a guide.
It's not a solution.
It's a voice one that sounds a lot like yours when no one's listening.
This book won't fix the world.
But maybe, just maybe, it'll make you feel seen.
And that's where healing begins.

CHAPTER I

Too Skinny to Be Seen

I didn't start life worrying about my body. As a child, I didn't even know what "body image" meant. I was just... alive. Waking up to the sound of my mother's voice, eating whatever she put on the plate, running around barefoot on sun-baked roads, sweating, laughing, falling, getting up. I never thought of myself as skinny. I was just me.

But the world has a way of making you aware of things you were never supposed to be ashamed of.

The first time someone called me "stick," I laughed. I didn't understand the insult. I thought they were being silly. "Why are you so thin?" they asked. "Do you eat at all?" I smiled and nodded because I didn't know how to respond. I didn't know I was supposed to feel bad.

But then it kept happening. More people. Different voices. Some laughing. Some whispering. Some pretending to care, while others were just cruel.

"You're all bones."
"Don't your parents feed you properly?"
"You look sick."
"You'll disappear if you turn sideways."
"You need to eat more, man. You're not a man if you don't have muscles."
"You're like a hanger with clothes on."

Suddenly, the body that carried me every day the body I never questioned became my prison.

I was rejected for the first time in my life because of how I looked.

I had feelings for someone. She was kind. Or so I thought. We used to talk for hours school stories, movies, random thoughts. And one day, I gathered the courage to tell her how I felt.

She smiled.

Paused.

And then said something that changed everything.

"You're a nice guy... but I just don't feel attracted. You're too skinny, yaar. I want

someone who looks strong... manly."

I said it was okay. I said I understood. But when I walked away, something broke inside.

I went home that night and stood in front of the mirror. I took off my shirt. I looked at my chest, my arms, my face. I pulled in my stomach. I clenched my fists. I tried to imagine how I'd look if I had more muscles. I tried to see what she wanted to see.

But all I saw was someone who was never enough.

That night, I didn't sleep. I didn't cry either. I just stared at the ceiling, wondering what I did wrong. The worst part?

I started to believe her.

It didn't stop at rejection.

My friends didn't say it outright, but they treated me differently too. In sports, I was the last to be picked.

"Too weak," they said.

"He'll break," they joked.

They laughed while lifting me up with one hand. "You weigh like air," they said. "Are you made of paper?" They called me "matchstick" and "skeleton" like it was the funniest thing ever. And even when I laughed with them, it stung.

I began wearing long sleeves, even in summer. I'd wear two layers to make myself look bigger. I'd avoid changing clothes in front of anyone. And I started googling:

"How to gain weight fast."

"Best food for skinny people."

"What to wear to look less skinny."

"How to get six-pack abs."

I bought protein powder I couldn't afford. I ate extra meals I didn't want. I did pushups at 2 a.m. in secret.

But nothing changed. My body refused to become what the world wanted it to be.

And then came the worst comment I ever heard in my life.

It was a casual conversation. A group of boys laughing, sharing crude jokes like boys often do. I didn't want to be part of it, but I stood there, trying to fit in.

Then one guy looked at me and smirked.

"Bro, are you this skinny because you masturbate a lot?"

The others burst into laughter. Like he'd said the most brilliant thing in the world.

I stood there. Frozen. A weird mixture of shame, anger, confusion, and humiliation crawled over me like ants on skin.
I didn't respond. I just walked away. But that sentence stayed with me.

It's funny, isn't it? How someone else's stupidity can become your burden to carry?

They say men should be strong. That boys shouldn't cry. That we should "man up" and not be bothered by what people say.

But tell me this how do you "man up" when your very masculinity is questioned every single day?

When the world tells you that being slim is feminine. That being fair is beautiful. That being big is healthy. That your body must look like a movie star's to deserve love or respect?

No one ever told me,
"You're enough."
"Your body is fine."
"You're not broken."
"You're not weird."

So I had to teach myself.

Here's what I learned, after years of silence:

I'm skinny because of my metabolism.
My body processes food faster than others. It doesn't retain fat easily. That's not a disease. That's not a disorder. That's biology.
And yes, it runs in the family. My genes were passed down to me not shame, not weakness, just a natural body structure that's been misunderstood by society.

I didn't choose this body. But I've learned to live in it. To respect it. To be kind to it, even when others aren't.

This body has carried me through anxiety, sleepless nights, heartbreak, loneliness, and self-hate. It's still here, still breathing, still walking. It's not less of a body it's my body.

And now, to the ones who called me names...
To the ones who rejected me without knowing me...

To the ones who turned my body into a joke, a topic, a "roast," a rumor...

Let me tell you this:

What you saw was a skinny boy.
What I felt was a human being trying to survive, trying to love, trying to live.
What I know now is... I was never the problem. You just couldn't see beauty in what didn't fit your definition.

But I can.

I see it now. In myself. In others like me. In every body that was laughed at, overlooked, and told it wasn't good enough.

And I'll say this loudly:
We were always enough.

CHAPTER II

Too Dark to Be Beautiful

This isn't my personal story. But it's one I've witnessed so many times that it feels like a scar on the soul of society. It belongs to people I know, people I've met, and people who never had the chance to speak out. So I'll speak for them.

It all starts way too early. Before you even know what skin tone means. Before the mirror becomes a measuring tool. A child, innocent and free, is born into a world that has already decided what beauty should look like.

Fair. Light. Rosy. Soft.

Anything outside that is "less than."

I remember a girl from my neighborhood. Her smile could light up a dull evening. She was always curious, always kind. Her energy filled the room before she even entered it. But when the aunties visited, they would pause mid-compliment.

"She's so smart... but so dark."

The "but" was always louder than the compliment.

She would sit silently as they spoke about turmeric pastes, sandalwood packs, and fairness creams. Not once did she ask for these remedies. Not once did she feel like something was wrong until they convinced her it was.

She stopped playing outside. She stopped smiling in photographs. She started keeping her face covered, trying to shrink herself into invisibility.

She was only six.

By ten, she already believed she wasn't beautiful. And no one had to say it out loud anymore. It was there in their eyes, in the way they treated her, in the way they praised other children who were lighter. It wasn't just rejection. It was erasure.

This doesn't only happen to girls.

I've seen boys teased mercilessly, too.

"Don't stand in the sun, da. You're already dark as charcoal."
"Which girl will even look at you?"
"You need to try this cream, bro. It works."

They laughed when they said it. But he didn't.

He started avoiding selfies. Started walking with his head down. Started avoiding any place where he'd be compared. He didn't want attention anymore, because attention only came with mockery.

We grow up in a society that treats fairness as a virtue. Look at the ads on TV how a fair face changes someone's entire life. From rejected to accepted, from ignored to celebrated—all in one tube of cream.

But no one talks about how many hearts those ads crush. How many childhoods they damage. How many lives they limit.

I have a friend who's now working abroad, strong and self-assured. But even she says, "I don't have a single childhood memory where someone called me beautiful. It was always about how dark I was. Even when I dressed up, there was a hesitation in people's compliments like they were surprised I could even look good."

Imagine carrying that weight for years. Imagine believing you must apologize for your skin every time you enter a room.

And it's not just people around us. It's in families too.

Newborn babies are examined not with love, but with color commentary.
"She's fair, thank God."
"Oh... a little dark, but it's okay, maybe she'll lighten up."

Lighten up?

As if melanin is a stain. As if skin color is a punishment that needs correction.

We live in a country of diverse shades of brown. But we still carry the colonial hangover that tells us only white is beautiful. Only fair is desirable.

It's not just about beauty. It's about worth. Respect. Opportunities. How people treat you, listen to you, believe in you so much of it is still filtered through your skin tone.

And it needs to stop.

Because here's what no one tells these kids, these teens, these grown adults who still carry childhood wounds:

Your skin is not a mistake.

Melanin is not a curse.

Dark is not less. It is not ugly. It is not something to fix.

It is rich. Deep. Powerful. Timeless.

You are beautiful not in spite of your skin but because of it.

So to the world that said, "Too dark to be beautiful"

We see your shallow standards.

We hear your silence when dark-skinned people succeed.

And we're done shrinking ourselves to fit your narrow view.

We're reclaiming space now.

What you saw was dark skin.

What I felt was rejection, judgment, shame.

But now, what I know is our worth isn't in your eyes.

It's in ours.

CHAPTER III

Too Fat to Be Loved

This one hurts in silence.

The jokes are always louder. The laughs are always public. But the pain? That lives quietly inside the chest of someone who's been called "too much" their whole life.

I've seen it far too often people being reduced to a number on a weighing scale. As if weight was the only thing that defined their existence. As if every other quality kindness, talent, humor, intelligence just disappeared under the layers of body fat.

They see the body before they see the person.

And the world never lets them forget it.

I knew a guy once funniest person in the room, the kind who could lift a heavy mood with just a word. But the moment he left the group, people imitated the way he walked. The way he sat. They mimicked his heavy breathing and laughed. I watched, ashamed, knowing he probably knew. People like him always know.

He once told me, "When I enter a room, I don't look for a place to sit. I look for a chair that won't break under me."

That wasn't humor. That was survival.

I've seen girls try on clothes in trial rooms and break down without a sound. Not because the dress was too small, but because it confirmed what the world already told them "You're not made for this."

Shopping becomes a battlefield. Eating becomes a performance. Love becomes a fantasy.

Because somehow, being fat means you're not allowed to desire or be desired. It means when you like someone, people joke about it. As if love has a weight limit.

I remember overhearing a group of boys once. They were rating girls from college.

"She's cute but fat. Imagine the bed frame breaking."

They all laughed. Loudly.

They never saw the girl who skipped lunch that day. Who googled "quickest way to lose weight" later that night. Who walked past mirrors with guilt instead of grace.

Do you know what it's like to be laughed at and expected to laugh with them?

To be the "funny fat friend"? The one who's always okay being alone, because apparently, they're not allowed to be the main character in their own love story?

People love to give advice.

"Just eat less."

"Try the gym."

"Have you checked your thyroid?"

"You'd look so pretty if you lost a little weight."

They say it like you haven't tried. Like you haven't cried. Like you haven't stood in front of the mirror grabbing your own flesh and wishing it away.

They don't know about the secret workouts. The pills. The skipped meals. The anxiety at family functions where everyone comments on your size as if it's public property. As if your body was created for open discussion.

And worst of all the shame.

Not just from others, but the shame you begin to carry within yourself. You begin to apologize for your body, for the space you occupy, for your hunger, for your dreams.

That shame turns into silence. And silence turns into self-hate.

But here's the truth:

Fat is not failure.

Fat is not ugly.

Fat is not the opposite of healthy, or beautiful, or worthy.

Being fat doesn't make someone less lovable. Less intelligent. Less ambitious. Less human.

Yes, health is important. Yes, we should care about our bodies. But don't use health as an excuse to bully, humiliate, or erase someone's humanity.

I know a girl who was once told, "You'd be a great catch… if you lost weight."

She smiled and said nothing.

But later she said to me, "I'm not a 'project.' I'm a person."

That stuck with me.

To all those who have ever been made to feel like they need to shrink themselves to fit into someone else's idea of beauty this chapter is for you.

What they saw was fat.

What you felt was rejection, humiliation, loneliness.

But what they never saw was your strength.

The strength it takes to show up every day.

To dress up even when you know the world will stare.

To love yourself when no one else is cheering you on.

You are not "too much."

You are not "too big."

You are not "too late" to be loved.

You are enough.

Just the way you are.

CHAPTER IV

But You Don't Look Sad

They say mental health is invisible.

I disagree.

It's just that no one wants to look close enough.

For a long time, I was one of them. I didn't believe in mental health "issues." I thought it was something people exaggerated. A weak mind. Too much overthinking. An excuse. A trend. A fancy label for people who didn't know how to deal with life.

Until it happened to me.

Until I was the one who couldn't sleep at night, no matter how tired I was.

Until I was the one whose heart raced in a calm room, whose breath got stuck for no reason.

Until I was the one who smiled in the group photo and cried in the washroom afterward.

Until I was the one who kept canceling plans not because I was lazy, but because I was scared.

Scared of people.

Scared of noise.

Scared of the what ifs in my head that never seemed to stop.

I didn't know it was anxiety. I just thought I was being dramatic. Sensitive. Weak.

Until it started affecting everything my relationships, my job, my sleep, my health. And when I finally reached out for help, I was told, "But you don't look sad."

That sentence broke something in me.

What does sadness look like? Is there a costume I forgot to wear?

No one knew I was waking up with dread every morning.

No one saw the way I chewed my nails till they bled, the way I avoided phone calls, the way my hands shook during conversations. No one saw the guilt, the fear, the fatigue of pretending I was okay.

Because I smiled.

Because I showed up.

Because I didn't want to be judged.

That's the cruel thing about mental illness it doesn't always show. And when it finally starts to, the world still denies it.

I live with anxiety disorder. I've also developed certain phobias of crowds, of loud spaces, of uncertainty, of losing control. Things that once seemed small now paralyze me.

A single phone call from an unknown number can ruin my whole day.

Too many people in a room? I'll find an excuse to leave.

A sudden plan? I'll overthink it till it becomes unbearable.

And yet, when I try to explain it, people say:

"Just relax."

"Overthinking too much, da."

"You need to be strong."

"Come out of it it's all in your head."

Yes. That's the point. It is in my head. That's exactly what makes it so exhausting.

Let's talk about depression.

Not the movie version. Not the slow-motion, rainy-window, sad-song montage.

The real one.

The one where brushing your teeth feels like a battle.

The one where you stare at the ceiling for hours, not knowing why you exist.

The one where you want to cry but can't. Where nothing feels real—not your goals, not your friends, not your future.

The depression that whispers:

"You're useless."

"You're a burden."

"You'll never be okay."

And then there's panic attacks.

Ever had one?

Imagine drowning in the middle of a calm room.
Your heart races like it's running from death.
Your lungs forget how to breathe.
Your hands go numb.
And you think: This is it. I'm dying.

But no one sees it.

You look "normal" on the outside.

So they say:

"Just distract yourself."
"Don't overreact."
"It's all in your mind."

Yes. Exactly. And that's the scariest place to be stuck inside your mind with no way out.

I've met people with PTSD Post Traumatic Stress Disorder. You'd never guess. Because they go to work, pay their bills, make small talk, laugh at jokes.

But a sound, a smell, a word anything can pull them back into a memory they've spent years trying to bury.

And then there's OCD not just "I like things clean," but the constant torture of intrusive thoughts. The compulsive routines they must do to feel safe. The fear that something terrible will happen if they don't wash their hands five times or check the door ten times.

And then there's bipolar disorder where you feel invincible one day and invisible the next.
Or schizophrenia where your own mind becomes a stranger.
Or eating disorders where control over food becomes the only way to feel alive.

So many conditions. So many silent wars.

And still, people say:

"Just be positive."
"Have you tried yoga?"
"Don't think too much."

Do we tell a diabetic to "just think positive"?
Do we tell someone with a broken leg to "just walk it off"?

Mental illness is not a choice. It's not a weakness. It's not a drama. It's not a lack of faith or strength or willpower.

It is a real illness.

And it needs real care.

You know what hurts the most?

When you finally find the courage to speak up, and people laugh. Or they get uncomfortable. Or worse they change the subject.

That's why most people stay silent.

That's why so many suffer alone, behind fake smiles, under "I'm fine" texts, beneath perfect Instagram stories.

But silence doesn't heal.

So if you're reading this and you're struggling please know: you're not weak. You're human.

If you've ever had to force yourself out of bed,

If you've ever cried without knowing why,

If you've ever wished to disappear not to die, but to pause life

I see you.

And if you've ever judged someone for their pain take it from me: I did too.

Until it happened to me.

Now I know better.

Mental health is not a joke.

It's not a phase.

It's not attention-seeking.

It's pain. And it's real.

And every person fighting through it day after day, silently deserves respect, support, and love.

Because what the world sees is often just the surface.

But what we feel underneath... is a storm.

CHAPTER V

The Man Who Wasn't Allowed to Break

"Don't cry."
"Be strong."
"You're the man of the house now."
"Real men don't complain."

If you're a man reading this, chances are you've heard these lines since you were a boy.

Maybe from your father. Maybe from a teacher. Maybe from someone who thought they were raising you right.

But all they were doing…
was burying your emotions deeper and deeper until you forgot how to even feel them.

From the time we are little boys, we are conditioned.
Conditioned not to cry when we fall.
Not to whine when we're scared.
Not to "act like a girl."
Not to be soft.

Boys are taught that strength equals silence.
That expressing pain is drama.
That softness is shameful.
That vulnerability is weakness.

So we suppress.
We suppress the tears.
The anxiety.
The heartbreak.
The fear.
The guilt.
The loneliness.

We laugh it off.
We distract ourselves.
We become "the funny guy," "the chill guy," "the ambitious guy"

anything but the broken guy.

Because if we show that part... we risk being called less of a man.

But here's the brutal truth:

Many of us are bleeding silently.

The boy who cracked jokes in class?

He cried himself to sleep last night.

The man who provides for his family?

He's drowning in debts, silently blaming himself for not doing more.

The husband who never shows emotion?

He's suffering inside, never knowing how to say "I'm not okay" because no one ever taught him how.

And you know what makes it worse?

No one asks men if they're okay.

Because the world just assumes... that they should be.

Men aren't robots.

We have breaking points too.

But when we break, the world mocks us.

When we cry, the world calls us names.

When we speak up, we're told to "man up."

And when we finally shut down, they call us heartless.

We're expected to earn more.

Protect more.

Endure more.

Fix more.

Sacrifice more.

And complain less.

We're allowed to lose everything.

But we're not allowed to lose control.

Even when the weight is too much.

Even when it's killing us silently.

I remember once, a friend opened up to his girlfriend.

He cried.

He told her he was depressed, anxious, and scared of failing.

She said, "You're a man. You're supposed to handle pressure."

He never opened up again.

That's how emotional suppression is passed on not just by men, but by society as a whole.

We are not just fighting the pain inside.

We're fighting the shame of admitting we're in pain.

Do you know how many men are suffering in silence right now?

Men who can't talk to their fathers because "that's not how we do things."

Men who can't express weakness to their partners because they fear losing respect.

Men who carry guilt for not being the "perfect son," the "ideal boyfriend," the "strong provider."

Men who think they're broken just because they feel too much.

And the worst part?

No one is listening.

Because society only reacts when a man breaks completely.

When he lashes out.

When he explodes.

When he disappears.

When it's too late.

So let's say this clearly:

Men deserve softness.

Men deserve space to cry.

Men deserve the right to feel afraid.

Men deserve to say "I'm struggling" without losing their worth.

Being a man doesn't mean you don't feel pain.

It means you've learned to hide it better.

But hiding isn't healing.

To the world that keeps telling men to "man up":

Stop shaming us for feeling.

Stop expecting us to carry pain alone.

Stop mocking our softness and worshipping our silence.

And to every man reading this:

You are allowed to break.

You are allowed to ask for help.

You are allowed to be soft, tender, confused, and emotional.
You are not weak. You are human.

The strongest thing you can do sometimes... is to be honest about your pain.

You've been carrying the weight of the world for too long.

It's okay to put it down for a moment.

You don't have to suffer in silence anymore.

But let's also talk about something even heavier.
Something no one wants to say out loud...
but every man feels deep inside.

What happens when one man does something wrong something terrible, like rape, assault, abuse?

Every man gets blamed.

Every man becomes guilty by gender.
Every man is looked at with suspicion.
Every man is held responsible for the actions of someone he's never met, never supported, never even knew existed.

Suddenly, all men are dangerous.
All men are monsters.
All men are threats.
All men must "do better."

The internet explodes with hashtags like #AllMenAreSame and no one even blinks.

But imagine the weight of that for a second.

Imagine being a man who has never disrespected a woman.
A man who listens.
Who protects.
Who stands against violence.
Who uplifts the women in his life.

And still being labeled just because you are a man.

You carry the shame of something you didn't do.
You face the hate for a crime you never committed.
You apologize for a system you didn't build.

That's not justice.
That's collective punishment.

Of course, let's be clear rape, assault, abuse these are evil acts.
And those who commit them must be punished.
No mercy.
No defense.

But hating an entire gender for the mistakes of one?
That's not progress.
That's another kind of prejudice just dressed differently.

And ironically, in trying to stop one form of injustice, society creates another.

The media blurs a woman's face when she commits a crime.
But when a man is accused even without proof his name, face, job, and family are dragged into the mud.

People forget: an accusation isn't always the truth.
And even when the truth comes out, the damage is already done.

He's already lost his dignity.
His career.
His relationships.
And sometimes... even his will to live.

This chapter isn't to defend men who do wrong.
This chapter is to defend men who do right but still suffer.

Men who are trying.
Men who are growing.
Men who are healing.
Men who are respectful, responsible, kind, but invisible in this conversation.

Why?
Because the world doesn't want nuance.
It wants villains and heroes.

And if you're a man, you're either a savior or a suspect.
There's no in-between.

To the world that blames all men:
Hold the guilty accountable.
But don't burn the innocent in your rage.

We can build a better society
not by generalizing,

but by educating, understanding, and working together.

And to every man reading this:

You are not what they say you are.

You are not trash.

You are not toxic by default.

You are not the enemy.

You are allowed to be angry at this injustice.

You are allowed to demand fairness.

You are allowed to speak your truth without shame.

Let this be a space where men aren't silenced by fear of judgment.

Where we can talk about our pain, our growth, our efforts... and our humanity.

Let this be the chapter where we stop apologizing for existing.

Because being a man in this world isn't easy.

And staying a good man... that takes strength the world rarely acknowledges.

But we see you.

And we're telling your story now.

CHAPTER VI

The Woman Behind the Smile

She walks past a group of men on the street.
Their eyes follow her like shadows.
Some smirk.
Some whistle.
Some say words that don't deserve to be repeated.
    She walks faster.
Head down.
Heart racing.
    This isn't new for her.
This is routine.
    From the moment a girl is born, she begins collecting silent scars.
Some given by the world.
Some given by her own home.
    "Don't laugh too loud."
"Don't wear that."
"Stay inside when it's dark."
"Be careful. Don't attract attention."
"Why are you friends with boys?"
"Girls don't behave like that."
    These aren't rules.
They're cages.
    She grows up learning that her worth is tied to how she looks.
Not how she thinks.
Not what she dreams.
Not who she is.
    Fair skin is beautiful.
Curves are attractive.
Boldness is threatening.
Ambition is arrogance.

She learns to survive...
by shrinking herself.
And when she starts to chase her goals?
There's always someone ready to question her.
"Did she sleep her way up?"
"She's too emotional for this role."
"Women can't handle pressure."
"She must be arrogant, look at her confidence."
A confident woman is often seen as a threat.
A silent one is seen as weak.
And a kind one is taken for granted.
It's a lose-lose game.
But wait.
When a woman raises her voice about abuse,
she's called a liar.
When she dresses the way she likes,
she's called easy.
When she chooses not to marry,
she's called arrogant.
When she succeeds,
they say she was lucky.
And if she fails,
they say women are not made for this anyway.
So what is she allowed to be?
Let's talk about something real.
Periods.
A biological process that half the world experiences still treated like
a dirty secret.
Whispers in medical shops.
"Hide the pad."
"Don't enter the temple."
"Don't sit on the bed."
"Don't touch the pickle."
Is this 2025 or 1825?
And motherhood?

Yes, it's beautiful.
But it's also painful.
Exhausting.
Sacrificing.
No one talks about the mental breakdowns.
The sleepless nights.
The guilt of not being the "perfect" mom.
Or the pressure of holding everything together without complaining.
And even if she's not a mother
She still nurtures.
Still gives.
Still holds everyone else while no one checks if she's okay.
Then there's social media.
Where filters turn pain into perfection.
Where women are either worshipped as goddesses or reduced to bodies.
Where every reel, every photo, every word is judged.
Too much skin? She's desperate.
Too little? She's boring.
A woman posts a photo for herself
and suddenly it's open to a thousand opinions, most of them cruel.
Why?
Because somewhere deep down, society still treats women like they exist for others.
But here's what the world doesn't always see:
The strength of a woman is not in her smile.
It's in the pain she hides.
In the dreams she chases when the world tells her to stop.
In the times she breaks down in the shower and comes out strong.
In the way she loves even after being betrayed.
She is not weak.
She's been surviving in a world designed to limit her and still chooses to love, build, give, and rise.
To the women who are tired:

You don't have to be strong every day.
You don't have to be perfect.
You don't have to explain your choices.
You don't owe this world anything.

Your worth is not in your body, your marriage, your kids, your job, or your followers.
Your worth is in your being.

You are enough.

Even when the world says otherwise.

And to the men:

Support women not because you have mothers, sisters, or wives. Support them because they are people who deserve dignity, freedom, and choice.

Listen. Learn. Speak up when it matters.

Don't just celebrate her on Women's Day respect her on every other day.

We've spoken a lot about what men go through.

But strength is not in dominating others.

It's in standing beside them equally.

Let this chapter remind us that feminism is not anti-man. It is anti-inequality.

And when women rise, the whole world rises.

Because a society that supports its women...

is a society that heals.

CHAPTER VII

The House That Hurt You

They say "home is where the heart is."
    But what if your home is where your heart broke?
    What if the place that was supposed to make you feel safe...
was the same place where you learned to hide your tears?
What if the people who gave you your name
also gave you your deepest wounds?
    No one talks about it openly.
Because we're taught from a young age:
"Family is everything."
Even if it breaks you.
Even if it silences you.
Even if it makes you believe that your pain isn't valid.
    We learn to respect elders,
even when they never respected our emotions.
We learn to stay silent,
because "that's how things are in our family."
We learn to carry the trauma
quietly, obediently
like a child trying to hold a suitcase that's too heavy.
    Childhood Scars in Adult Bodies
    You grow up.
You move out.
But somehow, the voice of your father's temper,
your mother's disappointment,
your sibling's blame...
still echoes inside your head like background noise.
    You laugh with your friends,
but when you're alone,
you remember how crying was treated as "drama."
You remember how your achievements were compared,

how your dreams were dismissed as "not practical."
You remember how you had to grow up fast
because no one ever said,
"It's okay to feel."
So many of us are adults now,
carrying childhood fears we never addressed.
Anxiety. Overthinking. Self-doubt.
Not because we were born with it
but because we were never allowed to feel safe expressing it.
The Silent Pressure of Being the "Good Child"
Were you the "obedient" one?
The one who never rebelled,
never raised your voice,
never showed your true pain?
Because you thought if you stayed quiet,
you'd be loved more.
Because deep down,
you were scared that if you made a mistake,
your worth would disappear.
So you studied what they wanted.
You behaved how they wanted.
You lived a life shaped by fear of rejection.
That's not love.
That's survival.
Generational Trauma is Real
They'll say, "We raised you, gave you food, gave you a roof how
dare you say we hurt you?"
But trauma isn't about what was given.
It's about what was taken.
Your voice.
Your confidence.
Your softness.
They were taught to be strong.
To suppress.
To never show weakness.

And they passed that survival mode onto you,
thinking they were protecting you.

But you ended up learning how to hide your tears better than expressing them.

And the cycle continues.
Unless someone stops it.

Unless you stop it.

You're Allowed to Talk About It

You're allowed to love your family and still acknowledge they hurt you.
You're allowed to want to heal, even if they say "you're being too sensitive."
You're allowed to create distance, even from blood,
if your mental peace is bleeding every time you're near them.

Being loyal to your growth doesn't make you disloyal to your roots.
Healing yourself is not betrayal.
It's bravery.

Healing Begins When You Stop Lying to Yourself

It's okay if you still cry about the past.
It's okay if family gatherings make you anxious.
It's okay if you're still figuring out how to forgive them
or deciding not to.

Healing doesn't mean pretending it didn't happen.
Healing means saying "Yes, this happened. Yes, it hurt. But I will not let it define the rest of my life."

You're not weak because you're wounded.
You're strong because you survived something no one else saw.

If You're Reading This...

...And your home was never a safe space,
let this page be your new beginning.

You are not your trauma.
You are not your family's mistakes.
You are not here just to continue the pattern.

You are here to break it.

Start slow.
Set boundaries.
Talk to someone.
Write it out.
Feel it.
Let it burn.
Let it go.
But above all
Know that your story matters.
Even if no one in your family ever told you that.

CHAPTER VIII

Chasing Success vs. Inner Peace

Let me tell you something nobody said when I was growing up.
Success is addictive.
But so is comparison.
So is burnout.
So is emptiness dressed up in shiny clothes.
We are a generation that romanticizes the hustle.
Wake up. Grind. Post a story. Smile through anxiety.
Keep running.
For money. For fame. For validation.
Keep chasing something... anything...
Even if we have no idea what we're chasing anymore.
Because that's what success is, right?
A fat bank account.
A car that makes people stare.
A job title that sounds foreign.
A phone with a logo bitten off.
A holiday that looks better on Instagram than it feels in real life.
But let me ask you: When was the last time you were truly at peace?
The Cost of the Chase
I know people who have everything
Luxury, name, followers, power
And still cry themselves to sleep.
Because the voice inside them has gone silent.
Because they traded their peace of mind for pieces of validation.
I've seen artists who no longer create,
because they started making content instead of art.
I've met friends who can't sit in silence for ten minutes,
because they forgot how to just be.

And I've lived that life too
Where every 'achievement' felt like a drug.
It gave me a high for a few days,
but when the applause faded,
so did my sense of worth.
The Lie We Were Told
Society sold us a dream:
"Be successful, and you'll be happy."
But they forgot to mention
Success without peace is a slow death in a beautiful cage.
Nobody taught us how to be content.
How to be proud without proving it to the world.
How to sit in a room, alone, and feel whole.
How to measure a good life by smiles and sunsets, not just numbers
and notes.
They told us to win.
But didn't tell us who we're competing with.
So we started competing with ourselves.
Until even our joy felt like a failure.
Inner Peace is Not Laziness
There's a myth that if you slow down, you're lazy.
That if you choose peace over pressure, you're weak.
But here's the truth:
It takes strength to stop when everyone is running.
It takes clarity to not chase what you don't even want.
It takes courage to define success your own way.
Some people find peace in mountains.
Some in music.
Some in parenting.
Some in painting.
Some in a simple cup of tea with no notifications.
Peace is not the absence of ambition.
Peace is knowing why you're doing what you're doing
and being okay when you don't always win.
A Note to the Dreamers

To the one working late nights, wondering if it's worth it
To the one comparing their path with someone else's success reel
To the one who's tired of pretending they're okay when they're exhausted inside
Listen.
You're not a failure for feeling overwhelmed.
You're not weak for wanting a break.
You're not lost just because your journey doesn't look like theirs.
You're just human.
And being human is hard.
But being present is rare.
Choose rare.
Let your definition of success include your mental health,
your relationships,
your sleep,
your happiness.
If you don't enjoy the journey,
you'll hate the destination—no matter how rich or famous it looks.
The Most Dangerous Trap
Let me tell you what scares me more than failure.
Success that leaves me empty.
A life where I win in public, but lose in private.
A world that claps for my achievements,
but forgets I'm still a person beneath it all.
We live in a time where people have followers, but no friends.
Careers, but no hobbies.
Dream houses, but sleepless nights.
A loud life, but a silent soul.
That's not success.
That's a warning sign.
One day, you'll sit in silence.
Old, maybe grey.
And you won't remember your awards or your likes.
You'll remember moments.
People.

Peace.
Laughter with no camera.
Hugs that didn't need a caption.
That's what stays.
So run, if you must.
But stop once in a while.
And ask yourself Is this taking me toward peace? Or away from it?
Because in the end...
Success is great.
But peace is everything.

CHAPTER IX

Love in the Time of Filters

They held hands tightly in public,
but barely spoke when the cameras weren't rolling.
They kissed on cue,
but slept on the far ends of the bed.
They posted romantic captions like "Forever mine,"
but forgot the last time they actually said "I love you" and meant it.
     Still, the world admired them.
Still, people reposted their reels, saying, "This is what I want."
     But what people didn't see... was the truth.
     I've seen it too many times.
Couples faking a perfect love just to stay relevant.
Just to fit in.
Just to avoid shame.
     It's so strange, isn't it? How in a world of so much connection,
we've never felt more distant.
How two people can be together in one frame and yet feel oceans
apart.
But as long as the likes keep coming and the followers keep growing,
we ignore the aching silence in between.
     There was this couple I knew. Let's call them A and B.
They were "couple goals" for everyone who followed them.
     Sunset reels.
Matching hoodies.
Candid laughter in vlogs.
     But behind those scenes,
she would cry in the bathroom after he mocked her body.
He would drink himself into rage when she didn't reply to a text
quickly enough.
They would scream, break things, block each other and then
unblock just to shoot a trending reel the next day.

Why?

Because breaking up meant losing the image.

Because they'd invested more in their aesthetic than their actual emotional health.

And somewhere deep down, they were afraid:
Afraid of being forgotten.
Afraid of not being admired.
Afraid of being real.

You see, social media has turned love into a performance.

We don't just feel love anymore.
We plan how it looks.
We think of camera angles before eye contact.
We think of captions before conversations.

We are not in love we are in a contract with the internet.

And in that process, we lose what matters the most:
Genuine connection.

You may think your fake "happy" post isn't hurting anyone.
But here's the sad truth:

It is.

There's a couple out there watching you.
They fought last night.
They're healing.
They're slowly learning how to love after trauma.

But after watching your picture-perfect reel,
they feel like failures.
They wonder if something's wrong with their love.
They think, "Why can't we be like them?"

You're not just pretending for yourself
you're misleading others too.

Your lies are becoming someone else's pressure.

Let's pause here and say it clearly:

You don't owe the world a fake relationship.
You don't have to force a reel when your heart is heavy.
You don't have to post a selfie to prove love.
You don't have to smile when your soul is breaking inside.

Being private is not a weakness.
Not sharing everything is not hiding.
Protecting your peace is not selfish.
And if your relationship is toxic if love has turned into control, if affection comes with conditions, if care has turned into criticism then it's okay to walk away.
No number of followers is worth your mental health.
To Those Couples Who Are Pretending:
This is not judgment.
This is a gentle wake-up call.
You don't have to pretend anymore.
If you're staying in a broken relationship just for social media validation, ask yourself:
What are you really holding onto?
Is it love?
Or is it the idea of love?
Be honest with yourselves.
Heal in silence if you need to.
Take a break.
Have real conversations.
Let go if you must.
But don't feed people a lie.
Don't become the reason someone else doubts their real, messy, honest love.
Love isn't what the camera captures.
It's what happens when no one is watching.
It's how gently you speak to each other after a fight.
It's how deeply you understand even in silence.
It's the small gestures, the raw apologies, the moments when pride takes a back seat and vulnerability leads.
That... is love.
And that doesn't need filters.
Let's start a new kind of couple goal:
One that's rooted in truth.
In growth.

In compassion.
In privacy.
In depth.
Because no matter how beautiful the picture is
it means nothing if your heart feels empty in it.
So if you're reading this,
and you're in love, or hoping for it someday
let it be real.
Not for likes, not for reels, not for the world.
But for you.

CHAPTER X

The Art of Letting Go

Letting go is not an event.
It's a process.
A slow, sometimes painful process...
of loosening your grip on what you thought had to be,
and accepting what is.
We live most of our lives trying to hold on
to people, to plans, to moments, to versions of ourselves we've
outgrown.
We tell ourselves,
"If I try harder, it'll work."
"If I wait longer, they'll come back."
"If I become better, they'll stay."
But here's the truth:
Some people will leave.
Some dreams will die.
Some moments will never come back.
And sometimes, no matter how deeply you loved,
you will not be enough for someone who doesn't want to stay.
And that's not your fault.
The Fear of Losing vs. the Freedom of Releasing
We're afraid to let go, because we think we'll be empty without
what we're holding.
But maybe... maybe we're not losing anything.
Maybe we're just making space.
Space for new experiences.
Space for peace.
Space for truth.
You don't have to carry everyone.
You don't have to prove your worth.
You don't have to stay in situations that are slowly breaking you just

to be seen as loyal.
    Letting go is not weakness.
It is courage in its rawest form.
    I've Lost Friends
    Some of them faded away slowly.
Some left with a goodbye.
Some didn't even offer that.
    And for a long time, I kept replaying what I did wrong.
Was I not enough?
Was I too much?
    But here's what I learned:
People outgrow each other.
People change.
And no matter how tightly you hold on,
you cannot force someone to stay in your life who no longer wants
to be there.
    Let them go.
If they come back with truth in their heart, fine.
If not..
It's still okay.
    I've Let Go of Dreams Too
    Some dreams weren't meant to be real.
Some were built from pain, not purpose.
Some were meant to lead me to better dreams.
    Letting go of a dream is one of the hardest things you'll ever do.
Because it feels like killing a piece of yourself.
But sometimes, letting go of a dream
is the only way to discover a new version of yourself.
    Letting Go of Versions of Me
    This one hurts the most.
    The version of me who tried to please everyone.
The version of me who thought love meant suffering in silence.
The version who tolerated disrespect just to avoid being alone.
    I mourned them.

But I also honored them.
Because every version of me, even the broken ones,
were doing the best they could with what they knew.
But now, I know better.
Now, I choose better.

How Do You Let Go?
You breathe.
You cry.
You scream into your pillow if you have to.
You write a goodbye letter you'll never send.
You look at the pictures one last time.
You forgive not always because they deserve it,
but because you deserve peace.
You stop chasing closure from people who were never honest
with you.
And then,
you step forward.
Even if it's shaky.
Even if it's slow.
Even if it hurts like hell.
You step forward anyway.
To Anyone Struggling to Let Go
Letting go isn't forgetting.
It's choosing not to let your past control your future.
It's choosing your mental health over your ego.
It's choosing peace over proof.
You're not a failure for walking away from something that once
meant everything.
You're not weak for choosing yourself this time.
You're not heartless for letting go of people who no longer fit your
soul.
You are healing.
Letting go is love
The purest kind.

Love for yourself.

CHAPTER XI

The Healing Power of Art, Music, and Creativity

Sometimes, words fail us.
Sometimes, our wounds are so deep that speaking about them feels impossible.
Sometimes, the pain becomes so much a part of us that we lose the ability to even name it.

But then, there is art.
There is music.
There is creativity.

And somehow, these tools these expressions offer us something words can't:
A way to feel when words fall short.
A way to connect when silence becomes too heavy.

The Silence Between the Notes

I've often wondered how music holds so much power over us.
You hear a song, and suddenly, it feels like it was written just for you.
The melody wraps around you like an old friend, and the lyrics strike a chord you didn't know was there.

I remember the first time I heard a song that made me weep.
It wasn't the sadness in the song it was the relief.
It was the understanding that someone, somewhere, knew what it felt like.
The music didn't fix anything,
but it gave me a space to be real.

When the world tells you to move on,
when they say it's time to heal,
but you still feel broken inside
music tells you it's okay to be in that space.

To feel what you're feeling.
To cry.
To grieve.
To be human.
It's the silent understanding of what we don't say aloud.
And sometimes, that silence is the loudest, most healing thing of all.
Art: A Voice for the Voiceless
Art is the language we speak when words fail us.
A blank canvas whether physical or mental becomes a stage for our soul's story.
A photograph captures a thousand emotions that never needed to be said.
A painting reflects every ounce of joy, pain, and passion we carry inside,
but could never express in simple sentences.
I've watched people pour their pain into their art,
and I've seen how it transforms them.
It becomes a process of unburdening,
of channeling their struggles into something tangible.
Through the brushstroke, the sculpted form, the written word,
art becomes their voice.
And in doing so, it gives them the strength to find peace.
Creativity: A Sacred Space for Healing
Creativity has always been a space of refuge for me.
Not just as an artist, but as a person.
I used to think creativity was about making something "good" or "beautiful."
But over the years, I've learned:
It's not about the outcome.
It's about the process.
The act of creating whether it's a film, a song, a drawing, or a poem becomes an emotional release.
For a while, the outside world disappears, and all you have is that piece of paper, that instrument, that tool.
For a while, you don't have to explain yourself to anyone.

You don't have to be anything other than what you are in that moment.
And that is incredibly powerful.
I've found that creativity often heals by letting you be honest with yourself.
It doesn't demand that you be perfect.
It allows you to express the raw, unfiltered truth.
And through that, it helps you build something that wasn't there before:
A safe space inside yourself.

The Magic of Self-Expression

There's a particular magic that comes from expressing your truth
especially when you do it in a way that feels authentic.
When you've lived your life feeling like an outsider, misunderstood, or even lost,
creativity is like finding a path that wasn't visible before.
I've seen people go from silent to loud through their art.
I've seen people who never spoke about their pain pour it into a song,
and then suddenly, they have something they can show to the world.
Not just to be seen, but to say, "This is me. This is who I am."
It's beautiful to watch someone who has struggled for years with their own self-worth
suddenly realize, through their creativity, that they matter.
And that they have a voice that deserves to be heard.

The Gift of Healing

Healing through creativity is a slow process.
It's not about finding a quick fix or a way to erase the hurt.
But it's about creating something from your pain
not to glorify the suffering,
but to make something meaningful out of it.
And in doing so, you slowly begin to reclaim yourself.

Sometimes, healing is not about moving on from what's broken.
It's about transforming that brokenness into something more.
And the beautiful part is creativity is always there,
waiting for you to show up,
waiting for you to give it your pain,
so it can give you back strength.
For Anyone Who's Struggling: Create.
If you're feeling lost,
if you're carrying pain,
if you're unsure of who you are,
I offer this simple advice: Create.
Whether it's through music, art, writing, or any other medium
create something that belongs to you and only you.
It doesn't matter if it's messy.
It doesn't matter if it's "good" or "bad."
What matters is that you took a moment,
and poured your truth into something.
You may not know it now,
but that act will begin to heal you,
in ways words alone never can.

CHAPTER XII

Love Isn't Always Enough – And That's Okay to Walk Away

They loved each other.

You could see it in their eyes the quiet smiles, the inside jokes, the way their bodies leaned toward each other without even realizing it. You'd scroll past their photos on social media and whisper to yourself, "If this isn't love, what is?"

But what you didn't see were the words left unsaid.
The nights they both turned away from each other in bed.
The pain that sat silently between them like a third presence in the room.
The sacrifices one made while the other took. The endless arguments that started with nothing and ended with everything breaking.

They loved each other. But they were miserable.

When Love Becomes a Cage

We've all grown up on a diet of stories where love conquers all.
Where heartbreaks are fixed by grand gestures.
Where pain is temporary, but love is forever.

But let me tell you something I wish someone told me earlier:
Sometimes love is not enough.

Sometimes, even when love exists, it comes wrapped in pain, miscommunication, unmet needs, and emotional exhaustion.
Sometimes love turns into dependency.
Sometimes love starts demanding things that hurt us.
And sometimes, love is just not the right kind.

You can love someone deeply and still not be meant for each other.
You can care for someone with every beat of your heart and still feel lonely next to them.

And sometimes, two good people just bring out the worst in each other.

That doesn't mean it wasn't real.

That doesn't mean you didn't try.

It just means... it's time.

The Guilt of Letting Go

Leaving someone you love is one of the hardest things you'll ever do.

It's like ripping out a piece of yourself and walking away from it, hoping it won't bleed forever.

People will ask,

"But if you loved them, why did you leave?"

They'll never understand that love isn't the only ingredient for a healthy relationship.

There's also respect. Safety. Understanding. Growth.

And when those things are missing, love becomes a band-aid on a bullet wound.

You'll carry guilt.

Guilt for not being enough. Guilt for giving up. Guilt for breaking something you once protected with everything in you.

But here's the truth you need to hear:

Leaving doesn't mean you failed.

It means you finally chose peace over pain.

It means you loved yourself enough to walk away.

Walking Away Isn't Weakness

We romanticize staying.

The idea that "real" love is proven by how much pain we're willing to endure.

But that's a dangerous lie.

Staying in a relationship that's tearing you apart isn't noble it's self-destruction.

Sometimes, the strongest thing you'll ever do is pack your emotional bags and walk away.

Not because you don't love them anymore,

but because you've finally realized you deserve a version of love that doesn't hurt.

A love that doesn't silence you.

A love that doesn't gaslight you.

A love that doesn't leave you questioning your worth.

Not All Endings Are Tragic

There's a misconception that every relationship that ends is a failure.

But I've come to believe that some endings are necessary.

Some endings are beautiful.

Some endings are quiet celebrations of everything you learned and how far you've come.

Maybe the relationship wasn't meant to last forever.

Maybe it existed only to teach you how you should be loved, or how not to settle again.

Maybe it helped you find yourself through someone else's reflection.

That's not failure. That's growth.

For Anyone Still Holding On

If you're reading this and you're stuck in a love that's become heavy...

If you find yourself constantly explaining, fixing, begging, shrinking

I want to tell you this with all the honesty I can give:

It's okay to leave.

It's okay to choose yourself.

It's okay to walk away, even if they didn't hurt you but just couldn't understand you.

Love isn't a cage.

And the one meant for you will never require you to lose yourself.

Because Love Shouldn't Just Exist, It Should Heal

The right kind of love won't make you question your sanity.

It won't leave you begging for attention.

It won't make you feel like a burden.

Real love is gentle.

It's honest.

It lifts, it frees, it nurtures.

And sometimes, the most loving thing you can do...
is to set someone free,
and set yourself free in the process.
    Even if it breaks your heart.
Even if the world doesn't understand.
Even if all you have left is a scar and a story.
    You'll heal.
You'll grow.
And one day, you'll find the kind of love that feels like breathing not surviving.

CHAPTER XIII

Nothing belongs to You

He was lying on the hospital bed, motionless.
Surrounded by machines, tubes, and the haunting rhythm of a beeping monitor.
His family outside.
Tears. Prayers. Regret.
He wasn't thinking of his bank balance.
He wasn't thinking of the temple he built.
He wasn't thinking of the people he argued with on social media about politics, language, or religion.

He was thinking of time.
Of what he wasted.
Of who he hurt.
And what he could've done differently.

But by then, it was too late.

We live in a world where people would rather kill than understand.
Where we're taught to hate someone because they speak a different language, pray a different way, or were born into a different caste.

And the worst part?

Most of us didn't choose our religion.
Or our caste.
Or the place we were born.
It was given to us.

So why do we act like we earned it?

Why do we carry it like a badge of honor and use it to divide?

A man speaks Hindi in the South, he's mocked.
A man speaks Tamil in the North, he's isolated.
A Dalit student excels, he's doubted.
A Muslim prays, he's feared.
A Christian worships, he's questioned.

A tribal woman seeks justice, she's ignored.
All because of labels.
Labels society gave them before they even knew how to walk.
It's like we're all wearing invisible name tags:
"Upper Caste."
"Lower Caste."
"Believer."
"Atheist."
"Urban."
"Rural."
"Educated."
"Backward."
And we treat people based on the tag...
Not the heart.
We've built temples worth crores...
But left hospitals gasping for funds.
We've fought for the purity of our language...
But forget to use kind words in our own homes.
We chant the name of God every morning...
But ignore the hungry child begging at the signal.
We post reels about peace and spirituality...
And the next minute, we comment hate under someone's post because they're from a different religion.
Where is the God in that?
Where is the humanity?
Caste wasn't made by nature.
It was made by man.
And now, it divides more than it unites.
Religion wasn't meant to be a sword.
It was supposed to be comfort for the soul.
Language wasn't meant to prove who's superior.
It was created to communicate, not discriminate.
But we've turned these gifts into weapons.
And the battlefield?
It's everywhere homes, schools, streets, social media.

People burn villages for religion.
Break friendships over language.
Kill over inter-caste love.
Abuse others online for believing something different.
All this hate. All this pride. All this ego.
And yet
we all end up the same.
A body.
Wrapped in white.
Burned. Buried. Gone.
No one takes their religion.
No one takes their caste.
No one takes their political opinions.
No one takes the likes on Instagram.
No one takes anything.
The only thing that remains is
What you did for others.
How you treated people.
And the memories you left behind.
That's it.
Let me ask you something.
What are you holding on to?
Your pride in your language?
Your caste?
Your religion?
Your belief that your God is superior, your rituals are pure, your identity is more authentic than someone else's?
Now...
Imagine your final day.
You're lying on a hospital bed.
Machines breathing for you.
The smell of antiseptic in the air.
Your loved ones outside, praying for another hour. Another moment.

And inside your mind silence.
Not a single thought about the arguments you won online.
Not a single memory of the people you looked down on.
Not even the verses you once recited with so much pride.
Just regret.
Of wasted time.
Of wasted love.
Of wasted life.
We are the only species that fights over invisible borders drawn by men long dead.
We slice hearts in the name of gods we've never seen.
We degrade one another based on the shade of skin, the name in a surname, or the language of prayer.
And what do we gain?
An illusion of superiority.
A fake sense of power.
But inside, we're all just scared.
Scared to be vulnerable.
Scared to say, "I don't know what's right."
Scared to admit maybe we've been taught wrong all along.
Caste. The curse that still breathes.
We hide behind culture. Behind tradition.
We say, "It's how it has always been."
But tell me does that justify anything?
A boy cleans toilets from the age of ten because his caste tells him to.
A girl is not allowed to marry the man she loves because his bloodline is 'lower.'
An entire community is considered untouchable, in a world that worships gods through touch.
Where is the God in this?
Where is the evolution?
We have phones smarter than us.
We've gone to Mars.
But here on Earth,

We still decide someone's worth based on the accident of their birth.

We speak of equality in interviews, post quotes from Ambedkar or Mandela,
but in real life, we still whisper about someone's caste behind closed doors
as if it defines how they should be treated.

Religion. The misunderstood sanctuary.

Every religion speaks of peace.
Of love. Of oneness.
But the way we practice them now it's all about division.

We don't see a person anymore.
We see their label.

"He's a Hindu. She's a Muslim. He's Christian. They're Atheist.
Oh, he eats beef. She drinks."
We stop listening the moment we place the label.

People are lynched.
Homes are burnt.
Children are orphaned.
Not for justice.
But because someone, somewhere, got offended in the name of God.

Do you really think God smiles when blood is spilled in his name?

Language. The pride that poisons.

Language is a bridge.
But we've turned it into a wall.

Mocking someone for their accent.
Looking down on someone who doesn't know your language.
Telling someone they don't belong in your land because their tongue sounds different.

Tell me, friend did your mother's lullaby not sound sweet, even if it wasn't in English or Sanskrit or Urdu?

Every language has its poetry.
Every word has its soul.

But pride without humility turns it into poison.

We talk about preserving language, but forget preserving humanity.

The Great Hypocrisy

We've built temples worth crores...

But left hospitals gasping for funds.

We've fought for the purity of our language...

But forget to use kind words in our own homes.

We chant the name of God every morning...

But ignore the hungry child begging at the signal.

We post reels about peace and spirituality...

And the next minute, we comment hate under someone's post because they're from a different religion.

Where is the God in that?

Where is the humanity?

And then comes death...

We are born naked.

We die naked.

We came with nothing.

We leave with nothing.

All the caste, the religious rituals, the linguistic pride, the blind beliefs they burn with our body.

When your bones turn to ash,

Nobody will ask what language you spoke.

What caste you belonged to.

What temple you visited.

They'll remember one thing

How did you make them feel?

So let me ask you this:

Why are you carrying hate that isn't even yours?

Why are you holding grudges based on ancient scripts that were never meant to divide?

Why do you think your religion needs protection from jokes, but your neighbor doesn't need protection from hunger?

Why do you think your caste makes you better,
when you didn't even choose it?
Why do you care so much about what name your god goes by,
and so little about the humanity dying in front of you?
We've been taught so much about how to worship.
But no one taught us how to be human.
This is not to insult your belief.
It's to remind you that belief without compassion is dangerous.
You can follow your religion.
You can take pride in your language.
You can celebrate your culture.
But the moment it turns into hate,
The moment it separates,
The moment it kills empathy
It's no longer holy.

A Final Thought
Imagine your funeral.
The people gathered won't chant your caste.
They won't play your regional anthem.
They won't hold a flag of your religion.
They'll stand silently.
And maybe whisper
"He was kind."
"She was generous."
"They were... human."
That's what goes with you.

Nothing else.

CHAPTER XIV

Rewriting Your Own Rules

They wrote the rules before you were even born.

They said how you should look.

They decided how a man should behave.

They defined what makes a woman "respectable."

They mapped out your life like a blueprint study, settle, marry, reproduce, repeat.

They told you not to cry, not to fail, not to question.

And for a while, you probably tried to follow those rules didn't you?

You wore clothes that didn't feel like you.

You smiled when it hurt.

You clapped for others when you were breaking inside.

You stayed in friendships and relationships that sucked the soul out of you because leaving would make you "selfish."

They taught you shame like it was a subject in school.

Shame for your body.

Shame for your silence.

Shame for your loudness.

Shame for being too soft, too strong, too sensitive, too sexual, too spiritual, too human.

And then one day... you broke.

Not loudly. Not dramatically.

Maybe it was quiet. A small crack in your spirit.

You sat alone and whispered to yourself,

"I don't want to live like this anymore."

And that's when it begins.

That's when you begin.

Not the version they wanted. Not the version they approved.

But you.

The rules they gave you? They don't apply anymore.

You don't have to get married by 30.
You don't have to work a job that kills your joy just to be "stable."
You don't have to be skinny, muscular, fair, tall, or flawless to be seen.
You don't have to explain your trauma, your silence, your boundaries, or your healing.

You don't need permission to live a life that feels like yours.
Rewriting your own rules means...
Saying no when your voice used to tremble.
Saying yes to things that scare you but make you feel alive.
Walking away from people you once begged to stay.
Making peace with who you are not when you "fix" yourself, but as you are now.

You get to redefine success.
You get to rebuild what love looks like.
You get to reimagine happiness.
You get to exist... without performing.

They'll still talk.
They'll say you've changed. That you've become selfish.
That you're doing too much or not enough.
Let them.

You weren't born to make everyone comfortable.
You weren't born to be liked by everyone.
You were born to live, deeply not just survive.

So go ahead.
Rip up the old manual.
Throw away the checklists.
Set fire to their expectations.

And write your own story.
Rule by rule. Page by page. Scar by scar.

Because at the end of the day when your bones are tired and the world has gone quiet —
you are the only one who has to live with the life you chose.

Make it yours.

CHAPTER XV

The Silent Battles We All Carry

Some wounds don't bleed.

They don't show up in blood tests.

They don't scream for attention.

They just... exist quietly.

Like a shadow that follows you everywhere even on your brightest days.

Every person you pass, every friend you laugh with, every stranger on the bus they're all carrying something they don't talk about.

Some are grieving people who are still alive.

Some are healing from families that never apologized.

Some are smiling through depression because that's the only way they know to be loved.

Some are still learning how to live in a world that never felt made for them.

We all carry pain differently.

Some people work 15 hours a day so they don't have to sit with their thoughts.

Some jump from relationship to relationship, hoping someone will finally make them feel enough.

Some stay quiet because every time they spoke, someone made them regret it.

Some laugh the loudest because they're scared of silence.

And here's the truth:

None of us have it all figured out.

Not the ones who seem wise.

Not the ones who look strong.

Not the ones who post motivational reels.

Everyone's just trying to survive their own version of chaos.

So be gentle.

Be gentle with your story and theirs.
Be gentle with your past and your future.
Be gentle with how long healing is taking.
Be gentle when you look in the mirror.
Be gentle when you fall apart again, even after promising yourself you wouldn't.

Because this is what they don't tell you:

Healing doesn't always feel like progress.
Sometimes, it feels like losing yourself again.
Sometimes, it's relapsing into thoughts you swore you were done with.
Sometimes, it's waking up and simply choosing to breathe nothing more, nothing less.

And that's okay.

You're not here to win at life.

You're here to live.

To try.
To cry.
To rest.
To get back up.
To learn.
To unlearn.
To become.

And maybe one day not today, not tomorrow but someday...
You'll look back and realize:
You survived things that tried to end you.
You softened without breaking.
You changed without losing your heart.
You lived truly lived and that's all that ever mattered.

So here's to the ones still healing.
Still fighting silent battles.
Still showing up.
Still rewriting their own rules.

Be kind to everyone.
Because you don't know their story.

And they might not be ready to tell it.
    Yet.

Afterword

When I began writing Whose Rules, I didn't have a map.
Only memories.
Only scars.
Only stories I knew needed to be told not just for me, but for everyone who has ever felt silenced by society's expectations.

This book is not a perfect solution. It's a reflection.
A mirror that speaks for those who didn't get to explain themselves.
And I hope somewhere between these chapters you found a piece of yourself.

Because your story matters.
Your feelings are valid.
And your voice deserves to be heard even if it shakes.

Thank you for walking with me through these pages.